Themes for Listening and Speaking

Themes for Listening and Speaking

Carole Robinson and Helen Parker

Oxford University Press

Oxford University Press
Walton Street, Oxford OX2 6DP

Oxford New York Toronto Delhi Bombay
Calcutta Madras Karachi Petaling Jaya
Singapore Hong Kong Tokyo Nairobi Dar es Salaam
Cape Town Melbourne Auckland

and associated companies in
Beirut Berlin Ibadan Nicosia

OXFORD is a trade mark of Oxford University Press

ISBN 0 19 432792 2
© Oxford University Press 1986

First published 1986
Second impression 1987

Illustrations by:
David Ace
Jill Downie
Simon Gooch
Joanna Quinn

Printed in Hong Kong

Acknowledgements
*The publishers would like to thank the following for permission to
reproduce photographs:*

Camera Press
Michael Cole Camerawork
Richard and Sally Greenhill
Christopher Moore
Jill Posener
Rex Features

Photographs by:
Nicky Dixon
Rob Judges
Julian Prentis

In addition, the authors would like to thank their advanced students at
Oxford College of Further Education.

Themes for Listening and Speaking is designed for all advanced students of English who need to improve their listening and speaking skills.

The book has been organized to give maximum flexibility. By consulting the Lesson Planner at the front of the book, it is possible to follow a variety of paths through the units, choosing on the basis of topic or linguistic criteria. Each unit is divided into three sections. The Listening section contains a task or tasks based on an authentic recording. The Practice section, which follows, provides exercises on functions, structures, vocabulary, stress and intonation. Finally, the Speaking section provides a 'free stage' with a variety of communicative activities based around the theme of the unit.

Lesson Planner

Unit	Mode/Topic	Speakers
1 Ladies and gentlemen	public announcement: at an international conference	American
2 An Aussie at Eton	interview: an Australian at Britain's most traditional school	RP*; Australian
3 While you were out	telephone: ansaphone messages	RP; American; London; advanced RP
4 A woman's place	conversation: a couple discuss suitable presents for men or women	RP; RP
5 Hard sell	radio: advertisements	American; American
6 What's my line?	radio game: people talk about their work	Irish; RP; Scottish; Northern; RP; Northern
7 Plain sailing	instructions: a teacher explains a sailing course	West Country
8 Till death us do part	conversation: three women discuss marriage in their cultures	Indian; Danish; Brazilian
9 Another country	interview: an immigrant talks about living and working in the UK	RP; Caribbean
10 Local government	lecture: a lecturer explains government and education	RP
11 Spot the sport	various: people talk about sports	Australian; RP; London; Canadian; RP
12 Eccentrics	conversation: two friends talk about unusual people	RP; RP
13 Dr Norton's surgery	telephone: a secretary makes an appointment	Midlands; RP
14 After a fashion	talks: two costume museum guides explain some exhibits	RP; RP
15 At a loss for words	conversation: discussion about the influence of one language on another	French; RP
16 Waiting in the wings	radio interview: an aging actress talks on a satirical radio show	RP; RP
17 Jobspot	local radio programme: details of job vacancies	RP; West Country
18 Help!	telephone conversation: a friend asks a favour	American (southern)
19 Coping	conversation: a mother talks about her mentally handicapped son	RP; RP
20 And later today	radio: a preview of the morning's programmes	RP
21 Fairground Dream	song: a girl falls in love at first sight	RP
22 What's on?	conversation: two young people plan a day at an arts festival	RP; RP
23 A Hollywood story	narrative: an actor tells an anecdote	American

*RP = received pronunciation

Listening	Practice	Speaking
note-taking	function: giving instructions	giving instructions
accuracy checking	vocabulary: collocation	discussing the press
taking messages	function: making suggestions; structure: reported speech	role play: a phone conversation
multiple choice comprehension	intonation	discussing an advertisement
multiple choice comprehension; cloze	style; stress	reading aloud
identification	function: withholding information	discussing job qualities and job satisfaction
drawing course on map	vocabulary: definitions	giving and following instructions on a map
note-taking	structure: phrasal and prepositional verbs	discussing marriage customs
matching; true/false comprehension	structure: question forms	role play: a newspaper interview
completing a chart	function: giving examples; asking questions	discussing education
identification	structure: tenses	role play: a spectator at Wimbledon
matching	function: talking about the past	describing a person; limericks
completing a message	style and register	role play: a secretary asks for time off
matching	labelling; vocabulary: suffixes	describing photos; discussing clothes
completing a grid; multiple choice comprehension	function: confirmation; vocabulary: word building	discussing language
multiple choice comprehension	function: interviewing	role play: a chat show
completing a grid	vocabulary: word fields	creating a 'jobspot'
multiple choice comprehension	function: expressing reservation	role play: favours
multiple choice; true/false comprehension	function: signalling interest	discussing problems faced by disabled people
proof-reading	vocabulary: collocation; word building	reading aloud
cloze	pronunciation	discussing pop music
checking	function: making suggestions; agreement/disagreement	role play: planning a social schedule
re-ordering; true/false comprehension	function: story-telling techniques	writing and telling a story

1 Ladies and gentlemen

Listening

A Below are Professor Hunt Williams's notes for the announcements he has to make at the final plenary session of an international conference on urban planning. Listen to his announcements and fill in the missing information.

B Dr Paul van der Sweep is a delegate at the conference, and has been attending the sessions on computer-aided building design. This morning he took notes of the discussion he attended. He is leaving the conference today and is booked on the 17.15 plane. He has always wanted to visit Hawaii. Tick (√) in the box provided, those of Professor Williams's announcements that are relevant to Dr van der Sweep.

1. Final discussion of urban .... will move to Room .... □

2. Domestic .... session will move to room .... □

3. Return .... to .... Lodge. □

4. Return discussion .... to .... by .... □

5. First .... for airport outside .... Building at .... □

6. Second .... at .... Delegates to arrive .... □

7. Drs Schapsinger, Garbeldi and Surmander: Collect .... from conference .... □

8. Dr Goldman (........... Institute) .....th Annual Convention of ...., in ...., in .... Interested parties leave .... at conference .... □

Practice

A Professor Williams is speaking in a formal, international setting, and his aim is to be very polite and clear. Listen again to the recording, and note down the words the speaker uses to do the following:

1 stop the delegates talking

... I ... have your ... for a moment, please.

2 make polite requests

(discussion records) I ... to ... you return them to the session chairpeople.
(coaches) I'd ... to ... you all to be there, ready for the buses, at least five minutes before the departure times.

3 repeat information

We're moving the final discussion to Room 201. . . . Room 201. Which means that the domestic shelter session will be changed from Room 201 to Room 304. . . . the domestic shelter session in Room 304.

4 finish relaying each piece of information

5 address his audience at the start and finish

B The speaker has to make six announcements. Listen again to the recording and find the words he uses to introduce each new piece of information.

1 (room change) Now, . . . , I'd like to mention
2 (return keys) . . . , I have a . . .
3 . . . to your discussion records
4 . . . coaches for the airport
5 I have . . . for Dr Schapsinger
6 (P.E.S. Convention) . . . , I have a reminder

Speaking

You are a tourist guide. Your coachload of tourists has arrived at its destination, and you have the information below to give them. Using some of the language practised earlier, decide where polite requests would be appropriate and how you would progress from one point to another. Make the speech.

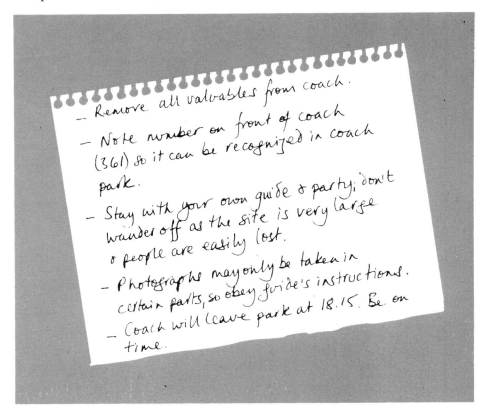

- Remove all valuables from coach.
- Note number on front of coach (361) so it can be recognized in coach park.
- Stay with your own guide & party; don't wander off as the site is very large & people are easily lost.
- Photographs may only be taken in certain parts, so obey guide's instructions.
- Coach will leave park at 18.15. Be on time.

2 An Aussie at Eton

Listening

ETON SHOCK REVELATIONS

Bronzed New Zealander Charles Marston rocked the boat at Eton College last week when he struck out at the £6,000-a-year private school. Charles, thirty, in a frank interview with hard-hitting radio personality, Milly Jarvis, slammed Eton and its traditions. And Charles is not the spoiled brat of an aristocrat, but a teacher at the exclusive public school. Headmaster Dr Raymond Birchett is said to be 'displeased' by Charles's disclosures.

CLOTHES TO GO

Charles revealed that the conspicuous uniform, familiar to residents of Eton village, and worn by both staff and pupils, was about to be replaced with 'something more normal' and he also talked openly about the exclusive Eton wall game and field game.

RUDE GESTURES

But the facts which are most likely to worry the £30,000 a year Head are Charles's frank revelations of the breakdown of discipline at Eton. Charles divulged that fights where the younger boys were mobbed by the older ones were a common feature of Eton life. And he admitted that boys frequently make rude gestures at masters. With these blatant examples of anarchy in the 400-year-old school, Charles Marston advised Milly Jarvis not to send her son there.

COLLAPSE?

These exposures came hot on the heels of the scandals recently revealed at Dartington Hall, another of Britain's high-charging private schools. Is this evidence that these last bastions of education and class privilege are fast crumbling? Charles Marston yesterday told our reporter, 'I have no comment to make.'

A A teacher at a famous English school gave an interview about life there. The article above, based on the interview, was submitted to a local newspaper by a student journalist. The editor, however, suspected that certain facts might not be right. He ringed all the points about which he was suspicious. Read the article where you will see these ten facts numbered, and then listen to the recording. On the grid below, mark (T) for true, (F) for false and (N) for no information.

1		2		3		4		5	
6		7		8		9		10	

B Listen again and tick (√) the correct answers in the boxes provided.

1 When the teacher says he wears 'perfectly normal clothes', he means the clothes he wears are

a ☐ ordinary.   **c** ☐ odd.

b ☐ in very good condition.   **d** ☐ comfortable.

2 When the teacher says that Eton offers games that cannot be played in any other part of the world, he

    a ☐ is using the programme for publicity.

    b ☐ has forgotten what he was going to say.

    c ☐ is being ironical.

    d ☐ is advertising Eton's positive features.

3 When the interviewer says, 'So you wouldn't recommend that I put my son down for Eton', she is

    a ☐ asking for advice on Eton.

    b ☐ stating the teacher's views.

    c ☐ enquiring for further information on Eton.

    d ☐ asking for his opinion on Eton.

Practice

A Look at the list of adjectives below that occur in the recording. Each of the nouns in the circle is paired in the recording with one of these adjectives. Listen again and link each noun with its adjective, then look up in your dictionary any words you still do not understand.

adjectives

first
ridiculous
funny
stripy
normal
secret
eccentric
blatant
rude
egalitarian
qualified
decent

nouns

terms
trousers
gesture
signs
(set of) equipment
clothes
collars
impressions
staff
tailcoat
society
language

B Use the list of adjectives and nouns to form different pairs, for example, *first language, first signs*. You will notice that many of the adjectives have more than one meaning. Use your dictionary if necessary and try to find at least two nouns to go with each adjective.

Speaking

In small groups, discuss one of the following issues and report back your conclusions to the rest of the class.

Group 1   Newspapers invent news.
Group 2   A 'free press' can never exist as long as we have politicians.
Group 3   Newspapers are unnecessary.
Group 4   Censorship is essential for the sake of national security.
Group 5   Newspapers have a right to distort the truth for entertainment purposes.

3 While you were out

Listening **A** Listen to the four recorded messages on Patrick Lechlade's Ansaphone. Put a tick (√) in the box provided beside the name of each caller.

1 ☐ Christopher Orton   5 ☐ Wayne Jones
2 ☐ Brian Tidmarsh   6 ☐ Antonia North
3 ☐ Sam Schoenberg   7 ☐ Marty Hunt
4 ☐ Jenny Pargeter   8 ☐ Joan Orton

B The keypoints of the Ansaphone messages were noted down. Listen again, tick (√) the appropriate squares, and complete the notes below. The first message has been done for you.

1

To *Patrick Lechlade*   Date *6th March*

WHILE YOU WERE OUT

M **s** *Antonia North* of *'Tutler'*

Phone No ....

Telephoned		Please ring	√
Called to see you		Will ring again	
Wants to see you		Urgent	

Message *Jenny Pargeter wants photo feature on V.I.P. Suggests lunch Brown's early next week.*

Operator ......*Jon*......

2

To ....   Date *6th March*

WHILE YOU WERE OUT

M .... of ....

Phone No ....

Telephoned		Please ring	
Called to see you		Will ring again	
Wants to see you		Urgent	

Message ....*In* .... *few days* .... *Staying with*

Operator ....

3

To ....   Date *6/3*

WHILE YOU WERE OUT

M .... of ....

Phone No ....

Telephoned		Please ring	
Called to see you		Will ring again	
Wants to see you		Urgent	

Message .... *not* .... *available.* .... *or* .... *change order?*

Operator ....

4

To ....   Date *6 March*

WHILE YOU WERE OUT

M **r** *Marty Hunt* of ....

Phone No ....

Telephoned		Please ring	
Called to see you		Will ring again	
Wants to see you		Urgent	

Message *Wants to*

Operator ....

Practice

A Listen to the first three recorded messages again, and note the way in which each of the speakers introduces himself or herself.

1 ... Antonia North.
2 ... Sam Schoenberg.
3 ... Wayne Jones.

B Read the note that Jenny Pargeter left for her secretary, Antonia North. Below are some of the words Antonia North uses to pass on Jenny Pargeter's message politely. Find the words to complete the secretary's sentences.

1 She's ... me ... you –
2 ... see ... you can do a photographic feature on a VIP.
3 Mrs Pargeter ... like ... you at the beginning of next week ... she's going away.
4 She suggested ... you ... to have lunch at Brown's.

Antonia

1. Please ring P. Lechlade.

2. Can he do that photo feature on you-know-who?

3. I'd like to see him early next week as (remember!) I'm off to Vienna on Wed.

4. We can have lunch at Brown's.
Thanks.
J.

Speaking

Student A
You are Jonathan Bell, Patrick Lechlade's personal assistant. Patrick Lechlade has left you this note. Using the language practised above, ring Antonia North. Give the message politely, and arrange a day, time and place for the meeting.

Jon
Ring Jenny P's secretary at 'Tatler'.
Can do feature if it's this month.
Free Mon. or Tues. for lunch, but Tues. better, after 1.00 p.m. Not Brown's - so crowded. Suggest Langham's.
P.

Student B
You are Antonia North, Jenny Pargeter's secretary. Jenny Pargeter has left you this note. Deal with the call from Patrick Lechlade's personal assistant, and negotiate a day, time and place for the meeting.

Antonia

1. Forgot to say — if Patrick L. rings, suggest Mon. 12.30 at Brown's. Tues. poss. but not Wed.

J.

4 A woman's place

Listening

This is a conversation between a husband and wife that takes place one Sunday morning. Read through the questions, then listen to the recording. Tick (√) the appropriate letter, a, b, or c, in the box provided.

1 At the beginning of the conversation Harry is
   a ☐ trying to sleep.
   b ☐ watching TV.
   c ☐ reading the newspaper.

2 At first Harry is
   a ☐ very interested.
   b ☐ quite interested.
   c ☐ only half-listening.

3 What does Anne feel about the advertisement?
   a ☐ amused
   b ☐ indignant
   c ☐ furious

4 According to Anne, the Superchef will
   a ☐ keep her in the kitchen.
   b ☐ save time and energy.
   c ☐ make Christmas happy.

5 The advertisement is trying to persuade
   a ☐ men to buy their wives Superchefs.
   b ☐ women to persuade husbands to buy them Superchefs.
   c ☐ women to buy themselves Superchefs.

6 According to Anne, an equivalent present for a man might be
   a ☐ socks.
   b ☐ a diamond tie pin.
   c ☐ a power tool.

7 What do you think Harry's attitude is to the Women's Liberation Movement?
   a ☐ indifferent
   b ☐ supportive
   c ☐ scornful

8 When Harry says, 'I don't see why she shouldn't be', he means she
   a ☐ shouldn't be in the kitchen.
   b ☐ should be in the kitchen.
   c ☐ should be having a happy Christmas.

9 Anne says, 'It's no use talking to you' because
   a ☐ Harry's not listening.
   b ☐ Harry's not going to change his attitude.
   c ☐ she knows he's not going to buy her a Superchef.

10 By the end of the conversation, has Anne persuaded Harry to appreciate her attitude to the advertisement?

a ☐ yes

b ☐ no

c ☐ probably not

Practice   A

1 When Harry says 'Hmm', his voice shows us that he is only mildly interested in what Anne is saying. Listen to the recording again and tick (√) the alternative which shows this intonation.

a ☐ ⟶

b ☐ ⟶↗

c ☐ ↗

2 When Anne says, 'Of course it would be useful, dear', she is pointing out to Harry that he hasn't understood. Which word does she stress?

a ☐ Of *course* it would be useful

b ☐ Of course it *would* be useful

c ☐ Of course it would be *useful*

3 When Harry says 'Yes, well, what about her?' he

a ☐ wants to know more.

b ☐ wants Anne to shut up.

c ☐ is surprised.

4 When Harry says, 'Well, you always give me socks, don't you?' because he is not asking a question, his voice goes

a ☐ don't you? ↘

b ☐ don't you? ↗

c ☐ don't you? ⌄↗

5 When Harry says, 'plaid socks, plain socks, green socks', are these the only socks she's given him? How do you know?

6 When Anne says, 'Harry, Harry . . .' with a wide pitch range, which of these could she say instead, with the same meaning?

a ☐ You do go on.

b ☐ Oh, you're so sweet.

c ☐ Do shut up.

B In the conversation, Anne and Harry express many moods. Using the categories below, put the appropriate letters in the boxes provided. Some moods are expressed more than once. Check in your dictionary any words that are unfamiliar.

a sarcasm   **b** humour   **c** irritation   **d** resignation   **e** ridicule

1 ☐ **Harry** Yes, well, what about her?
2 ☐ **Harry** Are you trying to tell me something, darling?
3 ☐ **Anne** No, of course I don't.
4 ☐ **Harry** Well, you always give me socks, don't you? I've a drawer full of socks: plaid socks, plain socks, green socks . . .
5 ☐ **Harry** She's going to switch this on and it's going to do all these wonderful things . . .
6 ☐ **Anne** With this marvellous kitchen aid . . .
7 ☐ **Harry** Well, I don't see why she shouldn't be.
8 ☐ **Anne** Oh, there's no use talking to you.

Speaking

Look at the picture above and discuss the attitudes and assumptions that lie behind it. Consider the following points.

Is the original advertisement intended to appeal to men, or women, or both equally?
What response to the advertisement is indicated by the graffiti?
What is your own response?
Can you think of any other advertisements that work in the same way?

9

5 Hard sell

Listening

A Listen to this recording from an American commercial radio station. Then answer the questions below. Where appropriate, tick (√) the letters a, b, or c, in the box provided.

1 What are the brand names of the goods advertised?

2 The first item advertised is probably
  a ☐ a milk drink.
  b ☐ for washing dishes.
  c ☐ soap.

3 The last item advertised is probably
  a ☐ an air freshener.
  b ☐ a fabric conditioner.
  c ☐ a shampoo.

4 The woman's voice is best described as
  a ☐ intimate.
  b ☐ sexy.
  c ☐ persuasive.

5 The advertisement's message is that the goods at the store are
  a ☐ good value for money.
  b ☐ priceless and high quality.
  c ☐ inexpensive but good.

B The leaflet opposite is for the Hepburn Theater's coming season. Listen to the recording again, and fill in the missing information.

Practice

A Listen to the Makeway advertisement again and find six words that are used more than once.

B Listen again to the woman's voice, and find those words that are stressed because the speaker wants listeners to take notice of them.

C Choose brand-names for the following products. Then compose slogans to advertise each one. Try to use the word *even* as it occurs in the recording.

floor polish   toothpaste   low calorie soft drink   air freshener spray

Speaking

Read the passage below silently and then discuss with your partner what it is and where you would see/hear it. Underline the stressed words and then read it aloud for your partner to check.

Colin's crazy clearance sale starts on Friday, 27th July. There are massive price reductions on furniture, carpets and curtain fabrics. You'd have to be out of your mind to miss it. Colin's crazy clearance sale, starting Friday, 27th July, at Colin's, in the Brunel Plaza, Swindon.

H E P B U R N
T H E A T E R

North 47th St. Seattle

These are just some of the exciting events planned for the
.... season.

The .... Choir

The .... Bananas

 .... and the Melbas

Opera ....

Entertainment for ....

Booking starts ....

Ring the Hepburn Box Office NOW on ....

For details and dates, see over.

6 What's my line?

What's my line? was the title of a popular BBC television programme. The aim was to guess the occupation of a person as he/she mimed his/her job. Play a similar game yourself by listening to six people talking about their work. Try to guess the occupation of each and select your answers from the list below. Write the appropriate letters in the boxes provided.

a	police officer	**h**	photographer
b	builder	**i**	ambulance-driver
c	vet	**j**	fire-fighter
d	actor	**k**	artist
e	doctor	**l**	cook
f	traffic warden	**m**	welder
g	dentist	**n**	plumber

1		3		5	
2		4		6	

Practice

A Read the transcript below and notice how the speaker gives clues about her job, but without giving too much away.

Well, when I saw the job in the paper, it said, 'Go out and meet people!' you know. So, I thought, 'Well, that'll be the job for me, really.' So I went out and I had a little look, and now I've got the job and I do like meeting people. But you're outdoors all day. You know, when the rain comes and it's
5 downing it, you don't half get sore feet. People expect me to be fat and horrible and old and pokey and I'm not like that at all really. I mean, I understand their problems, you know. They come up to me and they say, 'Well, there's double yellow lines everywhere.' 'Well,' I say, 'I know it's difficult, I mean, what with the traffic jams and all that,' and I say, 'Well, I'll
10 give you five minutes, just five minutes, love, and then you'll have to be off and on your way, all right?' And some of them think I'm a little Hitler, but I'm not.

1 use of pronouns
In line 7, 'they' refers to the drivers. Can you find some other examples of similar use of pronouns?

2 being imprecise
In line 10, 'five minutes' are to do what? The speaker doesn't state what the five minutes are for. Find other examples.

3 choice of words
The speaker gives clues by using words associated with traffic, such as 'yellow lines'. Find another example.

B Read the job description below.

I'm a chef. You only have to look at me to realize my problem. I'm always tasting the food I cook. I have very long working hours as I start around 11 a.m. and hardly ever get home before midnight. I never get fed up with cooking because I'm always inventing new recipes. Often the customers ask me to come into the restaurant to tell me how much they've enjoyed their meal. That makes it all worthwhile. By the way, my wife never lets me into the kitchen at home.

Remembering what you did in the previous exercise, rewrite this paragraph, trying to make his job less obvious.

Speaking

A Look at the pictures above. Discuss with your partner the qualities you think a person would need to be successful in each job.

B What aspects of a job would give you most satisfaction? Discuss with your partner and arrange the following in your order of preference.

making money	variety in your work	challenge
meeting people	social status	being your own boss
helping others	security	opportunity to travel

7 Plain sailing

Listening

It is the last day of a week's sailing course. All the participants are expected to take a test to prove their ability to sail a boat competently. Each person has a sketch map on which to draw in the course. Listen to the instructor giving the directions, and draw in the course on the map below.

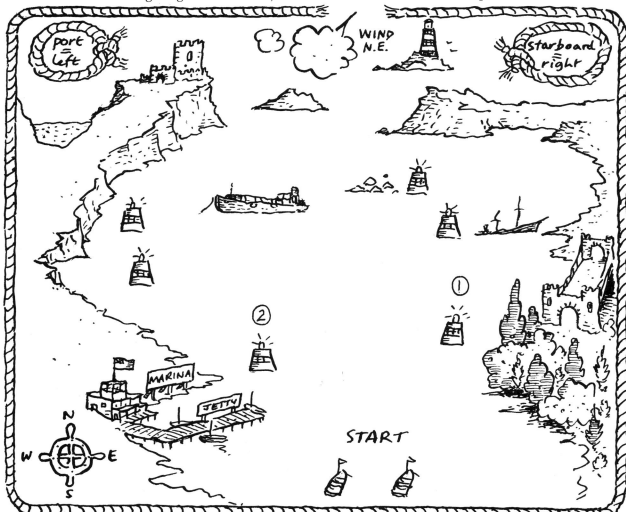

Practice

A Below are definitions of words the instructor uses that have to do with boats and water. Listen to the recording again and find the words.

1 river mouth
2 regular rise and fall in the level of the sea
3 small motor-boat used on rivers and lakes
4 floating secured object used as a marker to warn boats
5 landing place for boats
6 boat that has been destroyed
7 large, flat-bottomed boat used for carrying goods on rivers and canals
8 tall tower which has a powerful light to warn and guide ships

B Find four expressions the sailing instructor uses to remind students what they must and must not do.

1 . . . your life-jackets
2 . . . as you go round the buoy
3 . . . that a boat on a starboard tack has right of way
4 . . . or you might end up one yourself

C Find two words the instructor uses that mean *go towards*.

1 . . . back to the wood
2 . . . for the wood

Speaking

You are in charge of a group of young people on an outdoor pursuits course. Today they are to be tested on their ability to read a map and follow instructions accurately. Read the country code below, then draw a route on the sketch map. Describe your route to a partner, making sure to draw his/her attention to the relevant points in the country code. Your partner should trace the route on his/her map. Check the answer, then change roles.

FP — Footpath
▪ — Public Road
FB — Foot Bridge
⊠ — Gate
PH — Public House
⚬⚬⚬ — Hedge
ʎʎʎ — Crops
⌂ — Fence
⊓⊓ — River
≈≈ — Stile
⊓ — Common Land

Follow the Country Code
• Enjoy the countryside and respect its life and work.
• Guard against all risk of fire.
• Fasten all gates.
• Keep your dogs under control.
• Keep to public paths across farmland.
• Use gates and stiles to cross fences, hedges and walls.
• Leave livestock, crops and machinery alone.
• Take your litter home.
• Help to keep all water clean.
• Protect wildlife, plants and trees.
• Take special care on country roads.
• Make no unnecessary noise.

Wear strong footwear and practical clothing. The countryside can be wet and muddy even in summer.

8 Till death us do part

Listening

In this recording, three women talk about marriage in their cultures. Usha, who speaks first, is from India, Hanne is from Denmark, and Lea from Brazil. Read the notes below which were made by a research student, then listen to the recording. Find the words to complete the notes.

Attitudes towards marriage in:

India:

Most marriages..........., but girl can.......... Weddings v. ....;
Size depends on groom's.......... in society. Even v. poor man has
.....guests. Bride's parents meet all wedding.......... Divorce........,
but v. ......

Brazil:

Marriage still a strong.......... among middle and upper classes.
Poor people just..............., and then.......... Nowadays,
wedding expenses.......... Traditionally, ... parents responsible.
Divorce possible since........, but people only allowed to re-marry
......

Denmark:

Until recently, most people just........together, and didn't bother to
..........,...... This presented legal problems when couple.........,
so now marriage becoming more.......... again. Ceremony - simple
..........wedding or..........office. Usually paid for by........
and/or............

Practice

A Because the discussion is informal, the speakers use a number of phrasal and prepositional verbs. For example, at the beginning, Hanne says that in Indian marriages the partners are *picked out* by their parents. She could have used the more formal *chosen*. Below are some of the phrasal and prepositional verbs the speakers use, but they are incomplete. Listen to the discussion again to find the missing particles.

verb	meaning
1 to put . . .	to unite
2 to work . . .	to be successful
3 to go . . .	to continue
4 to hang . . .	to wait aimlessly
5 to depend . . .	to relate to
6 to move . . .	to begin to share a house
7 to split . . .	to separate
8 to live . . .	to share a house as husband and wife

B Look at the words below which have to do with weddings in Britain. Use your dictionary to check any words you do not know, then label the picture and complete the newspaper announcement.

people	things	events
clergyman	train	honeymoon
bridegroom	headdress	reception
bride	veil	ceremony
bridesmaid(s)	bouquet	
best man	church	

WEDDING ANNOUNCEMENT

Miss Sharon Jane Griffiths, of School Road, Leafield, was ... to Mr Colin Weeks of London at St Mary's ..., Leafield. The ... parents are Mr and Mrs John Griffiths, of Leafield, and the ... is the son of Mr Daniel Weeks and the late Mrs Weeks.

The ... ... was Mr Julian Weeks, and the ... was attended by ... Tracey Weeks and Julie Hicks. The ... was conducted by Rev David Wise and the ... was held at Leafield Village Hall. The newlyweds are spending their ... in the Canary Islands.

Speaking

Discuss the differences between marriages in India, Denmark and Brazil, and explain to your group how they compare to your own country's customs.

17

Listening

A Read the questions below, then listen to Berresford Lewis talking about his life in Britain, in 1985. Draw a line linking the relevant date to the event in Berry's life. The first one has been done for you as an example.

1932	is caretaker at college
1960	left British Leyland
1971	left St Vincent
1980	born
1985	left bakery

B In the box provided, mark (T) for true, (F) for false and (N) for no information for the following statements.

1 ☐ Berry regularly works in the evening.
2 ☐ Berry liked England as soon as he arrived there.
3 ☐ Berry applied for a job in Oxford from the West Indies.
4 ☐ Berry was made redundant by British Leyland.
5 ☐ Berry lives some distance from his present job.
6 ☐ Berry sells cosmetics in a shop.
7 ☐ Berry is married.
8 ☐ Berry has two children.

C In the boxes provided, tick (√) those tasks which Berry's caretaking job involves.

1 ☐ redecorating rooms
2 ☐ selling cosmetics
3 ☐ seeing to the needs of the lecturers
4 ☐ helping with the staff nursery
5 ☐ locking and unlocking doors

D Tick (√) the qualities which *you* think apply to Berry.

1 ☐ charming
2 ☐ shy
3 ☐ unsociable
4 ☐ lazy
5 ☐ talkative
6 ☐ generous
7 ☐ good-humoured
8 ☐ genial

Practice

A Listen to the recording again, paying particular attention to the interviewer's questions. Look at the exercise below, and find the words to complete the sentences.

1 What do you ... do?
2 So you work shifts, ...?
3 And when ... you first ... to England?
4 And how did you find ... to England?
5 ... did you come to Oxford?
6 So what did you do when you first ... then?
7 ... you ... a job to come to?
8 ... your first job?
9 And why did you ... there?
10 You live just round the corner, ...?
11 I hear that you sell cosmetics there too. ... rather unusual, ...?
12 ... do you ... sell it to them?
13 So you ... do any demonstrations, or anything like that?
14 So how long ... doing that then?
15 ..., you're helping her to sell?

B Below are some of the types of questions the interviewer uses. For each type, find one more example.

1 'Wh-' questions (*who, what, why, when, where* and *how*) in the simple present:
So how do you actually sell it to them? (Q12)

2 'Wh-' questions in the simple past:
What did you do when you first came then? (Q6)

3 Tag questions:
That's rather unusual, isn't it? (Q11)

4 Questions with statement structure:
So really, you're helping her to sell? (Q15)

Speaking

Student A

You are a journalist covering the 1988 Presidential nominations in the USA. You have been granted an interview with Georgina Romoli, a strong contender for the Democratic nomination. Read her bio-data below, and decide on the areas you would like to question her about. Then interview her.

```
Georgina Romoli

Born in Kansas City in 1936.  One of five children of Italian
immigrant parents.  Strong Catholic family.  Father died when
she was eight.  Mother factory worker (clothing industry) - paid
for Georgina's education.
1959 graduated from Columbia University.
Worked as high school teacher in Kansas City while studying
law at night school.
1961, before graduating from law school, married property developer
Ernest Chiaro.  He provided financial backing for her political career.
Had three children.
1979 elected as Democratic Member of Congress for the borough of King's,
Kansas City.
Vice Presidential candidate for 1984 Presidential elections.
Democratic ticket failed to win.
Regarded as strong contender for Democratic Presidential nomination
in 1988.  Strong on domestic policy but inexperienced in foreign affairs.
```

Student B

You are Georgina Romoli, a strong contender for the Democratic Presidential nomination. Study the bio-data above, and fill in some of the biographical gaps in order to prepare for your interview with a foreign journalist. Think about the issues listed below.

your role as representative of women (53% of voters in the USA)
how your career has developed
the experience you already have that would fit you for the job
the further experience you need to convince voters of your competence
your social and religious background
your husband
your children

10 Local government

Listening

You will hear part of a lecture on the organization of local government in England and Wales. Listen to the recording and complete the chart below.

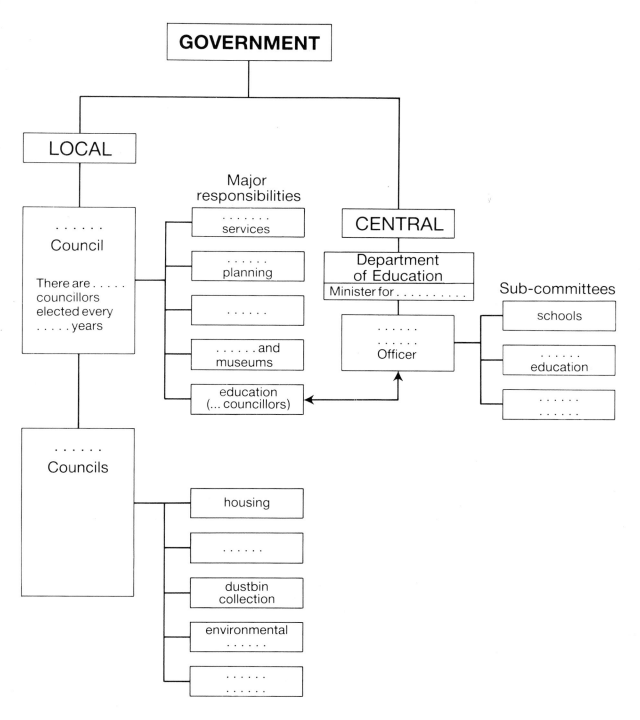

Practice

A A lecturer usually begins by making a general statement, and often follows this with an example. Some ways of linking a statement and an example are listed below.

such as
as shown by
as demonstrated by
for example (e.g.)
a case in point

Listen to the recording again and find the words the speaker uses in the sentences below to introduce examples.

1 If I ... of Oxfordshire.
2 ... they are building an ice rink in the middle of the city.
3 If we ... about the question of education.
4 I think this ... the idea of local government in the best way possible.
5 If we ... of Oxfordshire again.
6 If I ... of some of the structure.

B Imagine you were at the lecture. Prepare some questions for the lecturer on points you did not understand fully or you want to know more about. Remember: ask politely, correctly and precisely.

Speaking

Talk to your partner about education in his/her country. Find out about the following areas and try to get your partner's opinion on them.

the role of the government
whether education is free for everyone
starting and leaving ages
pre-school facilities
types of schools for different age-groups
exam systems
curriculum
streaming and mixed-ability classes
pupil power

11 Spot the sport

Listening

A Listen to the recording of five short extracts all relating to different sports and decide which of the following each one is. Fill in the appropriate letter in the top row of boxes.

a sports commentary   **d** announcement
b conversation   **e** broadcast interview
c speech   **f** news broadcast

B Listen to the recording again and identify each sport. Select your answers from the list below. Fill in the appropriate letter in the bottom row of boxes.

extract 1	extract 2	extract 3	extract 4	extract 5

g basket ball   **m** hockey
h rowing   **n** tennis
i athletics   **o** wind-surfing
j cricket   **p** show-jumping
k football   **q** table-tennis
l horse-racing   **r** swimming

Practice

A Listen to the fifth recording again and pay particular attention to the verbs. Find the words to complete the transcription below, which starts about halfway through the recording. What are the two tenses that are contrasted?

She . . . the wall – oh, and they . . . . She, she . . ., she . . . a brick but it . . ., oh! And another tight turn – and . . . the last – oh dear! She . . . that completely wrong.

B Listen to the third recording again. Find the two different tenses that are contrasted and give two examples of each.

23

Speaking

DRAMA ON CENTRE COURT

Yesterday, Wimbledon's Centre Court was once again the centre of controversy. The capacity crowd rose to their feet to take the part of petite Lourdes Ferreira of Brazil, seeded number 15, pitted against New Zealand's white hot hope for the championship, number 4 seed, Valerie Hursthouse.

Problems started when 22 year old Miss Hursthouse served a double fault in a crucial game in the first set. A section of the crowd, which had clearly been rooting for the young Brazilian throughout the match, cheered exuberantly. Miss Hursthouse, seeded number one in her home country, swore loudly and complained in no uncertain manner to the umpire. She continued to do this every time the nimble Miss Ferreira won a hard-fought point.

For the crowd, the crunch came in the third set when Miss Hursthouse disputed a line call. Frustration and bad temper exploded as Miss Hursthouse hurled her racquet at her startled opponent, who narrowly escaped a blow. Boos and hisses rang from the usually well-mannered Wimbledon crowd, with individuals rising to their feet and demanding that the umpire stop the match. The Duchess of Kent, watching from the Royal Box, looked more than disconcerted at the uproar. Miss Hursthouse was eventually led sobbing from the court by her coach, Andrea Spanberg, and a bewildered Miss Ferreira packed up her racquets to the encouraging cheers of the crowd.

Student A
You have read the report on the Wimbledon match, and know that your friend was among the spectators there. Question him/her about it.

Student B
You were present at the incident outlined in the article. Talk to your partner about the experience.

12 Eccentrics

Listening

This is a conversation between two friends, Helen and Carole, who are chatting about four eccentrics they have met or seen. Look at the pictures carefully. Listen to the recording and put a tick (✓) in the box beside each of the four people who are described.

Practice

A Read through the exercises below, then listen to the recording again. Find two ways Helen says she remembers the old lady well.

1 I had . . . of her.
2 I always . . . of her.

B Find two phrases Helen uses to say how much she liked the people she is describing.

1 I really . . . .
2 The character . . . .

C When Helen is talking about what the old lady did in the past, she uses the structure *used to*, e.g. *she used to ride a tricycle.* Carole uses a different structure for the same concept, when describing the habits of the woman in the British Museum. Find the structure Carole uses.

Speaking

A Describe an interesting relative of yours to a partner. Consider the following points:

looks
behaviour
personality
interests
any particular incident you associate with that person

B The following kind of rhythmic and humorous poem is known as a limerick. Read it aloud, paying careful attention to the stress.

There wàs an old màn of Perù
Who drèamt he was èating his shòe.
He wòke in the nìght
In a tèrrible frìght,
And fòund it was pèrfectly trùe.

Now make up a limerick of your own. It can be as silly as you like. Begin with one of the sentences below.

● There was a young girl of Hong Kong . . .

● There was a young man called Bright . . .

● There once was a man called Ted . . .

13 Dr Norton's surgery

Listening

This is a telephone conversation between a secretary and a doctor's receptionist in a health centre. Listen to the recording and complete the message below from the secretary to her boss.

MEMORANDUM   TO .... FROM........... Angela ....

Subject .... Date .... 23rd March ....

Arranged appointment re .... vaccination for ....
at .... with Dr .... (Dr .... ill).
Remember to take .... Cost: ....
Signature .... *Angela* ....

Practice

In a formal context, we often have to be outwardly polite, although we may be feeling annoyed or impatient. Read the thoughts in the bubbles and then listen to the recording again. Match up what the secretary or receptionist is thinking with what she actually says. Put the number in the appropriate bubble.

1 I'd like to make an appointment today or tomorrow.

2 I'm afraid Dr Norton's not well himself and we're very booked up today.

3 Oh dear!

4 It is rather urgent.

5 Could he possibly see someone on Thursday?

6 Oh fine.

7 Yes. Yes, thank you.

8 Thank you very much indeed for your trouble.

Speaking

With a partner, act out a dialogue based on the thoughts below between a secretary and her boss. Before you start, consider the relationship between the secretary and her boss, that a favour is being asked, and the kind of language each would use. The secretary should be very polite in order to get what she wants, but should not tell her boss everything. For example, she would probably say, 'I have a family problem', rather than, 'I want to see my boyfriend'.

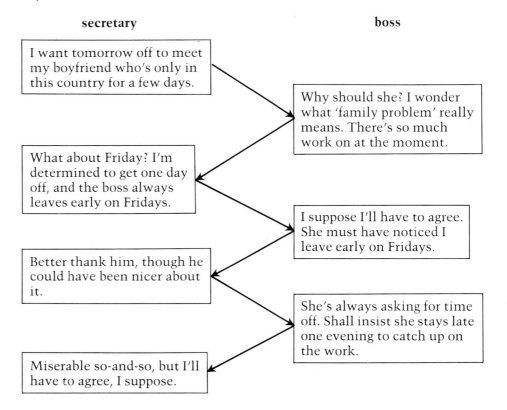

secretary

I want tomorrow off to meet my boyfriend who's only in this country for a few days.

What about Friday? I'm determined to get one day off, and the boss always leaves early on Fridays.

Better thank him, though he could have been nicer about it.

Miserable so-and-so, but I'll have to agree, I suppose.

boss

Why should she? I wonder what 'family problem' really means. There's so much work on at the moment.

I suppose I'll have to agree. She must have noticed I leave early on Fridays.

She's always asking for time off. Shall insist she stays late one evening to catch up on the work.

14 After a fashion

Listening

In this recording, two guides who work in a costume museum are showing a group of visitors around. They are describing costumes from four different periods. Put a tick (√) in the top box provided, for the costumes described. In the lower box, write the approximate date at which the clothes were worn.

Practice

A Listen to the recording again, and label as many parts of the costumes as you can. Use only the drawings mentioned in the recording. The more specialized words used are listed below.

parts of garments	supports	materials and decorations
overdress	frame	embroidery
underskirt	cage	lace
stomacher	pannier	trimming
headdress		feathers
frilled petticoat		muslin

B

1 Many verbs in English end in the suffix *-ate*. There are three in this recording. Listen again and try to find those verbs.

2 Look up the verb *imitate* in your dictionary and find the suffix to form the noun meaning *a person who imitates*. All verbs ending in *-ate* use the same ending. Form the nouns for the following:

a person who manipulates   a person who investigates
a person who demonstrates   a person who commentates

3 Using your dictionary to help you, find the endings of the following verbs. They end in *-ate*, *-ute*, or *-ish*.

| deterior- | comm- | establ- | distingu- | poll- | evacu- | toler- | imit- |
| flour- | demol- | exec- | ref- | anticip- | disp- | implic- | dimin- |

Speaking

A It is the year 2050. You are a costume museum guide. Look at the photos below and describe the clothes worn in the mid 1980s.

B In your group, discuss the significance of clothes. Think about the following areas.

wealth and fashion   dressing for work
developed and developing countries   clothes as a form of self-expression

15 At a loss for words

Listening   **A** In this recording, Alexandre and Carole are talking about the use of English words in French. According to them, these words fall into four categories. Listen to their conversation to complete the table below.

Categories	Example 1	Example 2	Example 3
1 No equivalent word in French	. . .	. . .	–
2 . . .	*speakerine* (means '. . .')	. . . (means 'dinner jacket')	. . . (means 'pyjamas')
3 . . .	*building*	–	–
4 . . .	*parking*	–	–

B Answer the questions by ticking the correct alternative a, b, or c in the box provided.

1 Carole and Alex are probably at the
  a ☐ airport.
  b ☐ hairdresser's.
  c ☐ dentist's.

2 When Carole says, 'Training means something quite different', she means
  a ☐ 'training' has a related though different meaning in English.
  b ☐ the French and English meanings are not related.
  c ☐ 'training' means the opposite in English.

3 When Carole says that English words are snobbish in French, her voice tells us that she
  a ☐ is surprised.
  b ☐ disagrees.
  c ☐ is impatient.

4 Carole thinks 'building' is an odd word to adopt because it
  a ☐ is so hard to pronounce.
  b ☐ has so many meanings.
  c ☐ has no elegant connotations in English.

Practice

A In informal conversation a speaker will often repeat points (his/her own or the other person's), in order to confirm and clarify what has been said. Listen to the recording again and find the words to complete the confirming statements in the table below.

Original statement	Confirming statement
1 There was a strong reaction against it	People . . .
2 We've got no word	It's often . . .
3 Snob value, I suppose	You . . .
4 It's such a mundane word	It sounds . . .

B Most verbs in English have a related noun. For example, *to think* (verb), *a thought* (noun). Many verbs also have a related noun which means 'a person or thing that . . .' For example, *thinker*, a person who thinks.

Look at the words below that occur in the recording and find the related nouns and verbs to complete the chart. Use your dictionary to help you.

Verb	Related noun	Related noun A person or thing that . . .
think	a thought	a thinker (person)
1 laugh	1 . . . 2 . . .	–
2 . . .	an expression	–
3 . . .	. . .	an announcer (person)
4 . . .	a reaction	. . . (thing)
5 occur	. . .	–
6 . . .	imperialism	. . . (person)
7 . . .	an example	–
8 . . .	a distortion	. . . (person)
9 borrow	–	. . . (person)
10 . . .	a building	. . . (person)

Speaking

A In your group, discuss the following issues.

Are any foreign words used in your language? If so, what are they, and why do they occur?

Are the categories of words that are distinguished in the conversation relevant to your language?

Is there a strong reaction to foreign words by some people?

B Discuss the problems that occur when a single language, like English, is used for international communication.

16 Waiting in the wings

Listening

Read the questions below, then listen to the recording of a radio arts programme. A famous aging actress is being interviewed about her life and career by an inexperienced journalist. Answer the questions by ticking (✓) the appropriate alternative, a, b, or c, in the box provided.

1 The play in which Dame Kitty first became famous was

  a ☐ *The Rat Trap.*

  b ☐ *Heartbreak House.*

  c ☐ *The Nun's Tragedy.*

2 Dame Kitty

    a ☐ took over Nelly Perry's part because Nelly Perry was drunk.

    b ☐ broke her leg because she had taken over the lead from Nelly Perry.

    c ☐ pushed Nelly Perry downstairs so she could take over her part.

3 Dame Kitty's autobiography was written by

    a ☐ Alex Smart.

    b ☐ a professional author.

    c ☐ Dame Kitty.

4 Dame Kitty's father came from

    a ☐ Morecambe.

    b ☐ Hackney.

    c ☐ Surbiton.

5 From the interviewer, we learn that Dame Kitty has been married to

    a ☐ an actor.

    b ☐ a solicitor.

    c ☐ a doctor.

6 Dame Kitty had a good working relationship with

    a ☐ Nellie Melba.

    b ☐ Nelly Perry.

    c ☐ Lester Guthlaxton.

7 When the interviewer says 'I beg your pardon?' he

    a ☐ doesn't hear what Dame Kitty says.

    b ☐ doesn't understand what Dame Kitty means.

    c ☐ is contradicting Dame Kitty.

8 The interviewer says the name 'Shakespeare' in

    a ☐ desperation.

    b ☐ disgust.

    c ☐ disbelief.

9 The interviewer says 'I think I just heard your five minute call'

    a ☐ because he wants listeners to know that the interview is live.

    b ☐ to shut Dame Kitty up.

    c ☐ because he doesn't want Dame Kitty to miss her entrance.

10 'Many happy returns' means the interviewer

    a ☐ hopes the play will be a financial success.

    b ☐ is wishing Dame Kitty a happy birthday.

    c ☐ hopes Dame Kitty will come back to the Theatre Royal, Morecambe many more times.

Practice

A Listen to the recording again, concentrating on the language the journalist uses to interrupt and guide the interview. Find the words for the gaps (...) in the following sentences.

1 **Dame Kitty** – but I'd just spent three months in a musical version of *The Seagull* so even then I –

☐ **Interviewer** ... fate ... and you took over the lead.

2 **Dame Kitty** Mark you , she hung on pretty hard to the bannisters.

☐ **Interviewer** ... a little ... how you came to take up a stage career.

3 **Dame Kitty** If you tell 'em your father was a respectable solicitor from Surbiton who –

☐ **Interviewer** .... Your first husband was a medical pioneer, I believe?

4 **Dame Kitty** Pour me another while you're at it.

☐ **Interviewer** ... theatrical career, Dame Kitty –

5 **Dame Kitty** The director hardly ever took his eyes off Romeo, they were always rehearsing the bedroom scene without me.

☐ **Interviewer** .... Dame Kitty, what part do you look back on with most pleasure?

6 **Dame Kitty** I managed to sink my teeth into that pompous old lecher Sir Lester Guthlaxton.

☐ **Interviewer** ... heard your five minute call.

B For each example above, put a, b, or c, in the boxes provided to show whether the journalist is trying to

a change the subject.
b keep the conversation moving.
c bring the conversation back to a previous topic.

Speaking

A Television chat shows, in which a regular interviewer talks to a well-known personality, are very popular in Britain. In your group, discuss why this is, and what qualities and practical facilities the host/hostess of a chat show needs.

B

Student A
You are a chat show presenter. Prepare twenty questions to ask a famous film star, but be willing to depart from your question list if the situation demands it. You must therefore listen carefully to your guest's replies.

Student B
You are a famous film star. Note down the main events in your professional and personal life, in preparation to be interviewed on a television chat show.

17 Jobspot

Listening

A This recording is from a local radio programme that is broadcast daily and gives out information about job vacancies. Listen to the recording and complete the chart below. Put a tick (√) where appropriate, or (N) for no information. Some of the information has already been filled in for you.

Job	Full-time	Part-time	Experience			Age	Pay	Hours
			essential	**useful**	**not necessary**			
hairdresser	√					. . .	. . .	Monday–Friday . . . Saturday . . .
. . .						. . .	£ . . . per hour	. . .
. . .						. . .	£ . . . per hour	Monday . . . Tuesday–Saturday . . . Sunday . . .
shorthand typist						. . .	. . .	. . .
. . .				√		. . .	£ . . . per week	. . .

B Listen to the item on the gardener's job again. Look at the chart below and complete it with the following information:

1 two tasks the gardener will be expected to do
2 two qualities the gardener should have

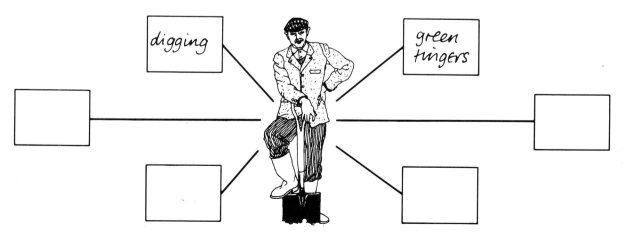

37

Practice

A

1 The gardening equipment below can be used for either digging, potting or watering. Join the tool to the correct box.
2 Name the tools. Some clues have been given.

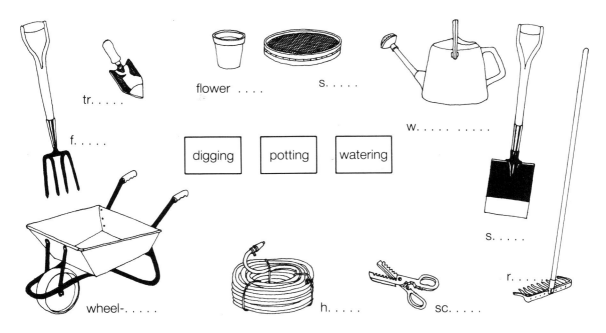

flower . . . .

s. . . . .

w. . . . .

tr. . . . .

f. . . . .

digging | potting | watering

s. . . . .

wheel-. . . . .

h. . . . .

sc. . . . .

r. . . . . .

B

In your dictionary, look up the words below that you do not know. There are four sets of four words. Each set is associated with a different job. Find each set, and the job associated with it.

saw	syringe	thermometer	bandage
plane	hammer	flex	screwdriver
spanner	wrench	jack	gauge
fuse	plug	stethoscope	chisel

C

1 Find an expression meaning *to like*.
2 Find two expressions the speaker uses to make a suggestion.

Speaking

With a partner, write a 'jobspot' so that each of the following people could apply for at least one position. Keep the style friendly and informal, as in the recording.

An 18-year-old girl interested in working with computers.
A 42-year-old redundant factory worker willing to do anything.
A 21-year-old graduate who can type and drive.
A 30-year-old man who has done a variety of jobs, is interested in working with people, but has no formal qualifications.

18 Help!

Listening

Liza receives a phone call from a friend. Listen to her side of the conversation and answer the questions below. Tick (√) the alternative which seems to you the most likely, in the box provided.

1 a ☐ The caller is offering to do Liza a favour.
  b ☐ The caller is asking Liza to do him/her a favour.

2 a ☐ The caller is going away on holiday.
  b ☐ The caller is going away on business.

3 a ☐ The caller wants her to look after a lot of things.
  b ☐ The caller wants her to look after a few things.

4 a ☐ The caller is asking Liza to pick some friends up from the station.
  b ☐ The caller wants Liza to look after a pregnant animal.

5 When Liza asks, 'Why do you keep them?'
  a ☐ she is indicating that she is not very happy with the arrangement.
  b ☐ she is thinking of keeping them herself.

6 When Liza says, 'I won't have to worry about it', she is referring to
  a ☐ food.
  b ☐ work.

7 a ☐ The caller is going to bring round a lot of carrots.
  b ☐ The caller is going to bring round a sack of fresh vegetables.

8 The conversation is about looking after
  a ☐ children.
  b ☐ rabbits.
  c ☐ cats.

9 Guess whether the person Liza is talking to is
  a ☐ male.
  b ☐ female.

Practice

A Liza commits herself wholeheartedly to the proposal at the outset of the conversation when she says, 'Just anything you want.' As the plan unfolds, she has to withdraw slightly and express her reservations. How does she do this? Listen to the recording again and find the words to complete the sentences below.

1 . . ., how many of them are there?
2 Oh no! Why, I'm . . . now.
3 Why, that's just a little too many. I mean, oh I don't . . . .
4 Well, I sincerely hope not. I mean, I'm . . . thing.

B Liza repeatedly uses three expressions to keep her side of the conversation moving, and to give her time to think. One of them is *well*. Find the other two.

Now listen to the full version of the conversation and compare it to the answers you chose.

Speaking

Student A

Ask a friend to look after your house or flat while you are away. There are a number of things you want your friend to do for you, but break the news gently. Some of the things you must include are listed below.

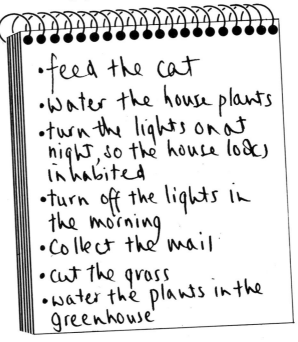

- feed the cat
- water the house plants
- turn the lights on at night, so the house looks inhabited
- turn off the lights in the morning
- collect the mail
- cut the grass
- water the plants in the greenhouse

Student B

A good friend of yours who you want to please, will ask you a favour. Agree readily. There may turn out to be a number of snags, so you will need to withdraw gradually. Play for time and express your reservations. You will probably reach a compromise.

19 Coping

Listening

A This recording is of a conversation between Teresa and Pauline, the mother of a mentally handicapped boy, about the problems and pleasures of bringing him up. Read through the questions before listening to the recording, then tick (√) the correct alternative a, b, or c, in the box provided.

1 Pauline
  a ☐ does not like talking about Andrew.
  b ☐ is willing to talk a little about Andrew.
  c ☐ is happy to talk about him.

2 When Andrew was born, the family
  a ☐ knew at once he was mentally handicapped.
  b ☐ knew immediately there was something wrong with him.
  c ☐ had no idea he was mentally handicapped.

3 The most frustrating thing for Andrew is that people
  a ☐ don't talk to him.
  b ☐ find his speech difficult to understand.
  c ☐ talk to him when he doesn't want them to.

4 Pauline's greatest worry is that
  a ☐ Andrew might be attacked by hooligans.
  b ☐ he will never be able to live on his own.
  c ☐ people may realize he is mentally handicapped when they see him.

B In the boxes provided, mark (T) for true or (F) for false for the following statements.

1 ☐ Andrew can dress himself very well.
2 ☐ Andrew is a sociable person.
3 ☐ Andrew plays some sports.
4 ☐ Andrew can travel around by himself.

Practice

A The sentences below have been taken from the recording but the words in italics substituted for the original words. Listen to the recording again and find the original word or phrase in the conversation.

1 He's mentally *subnormal*.
2 I'm sorry. I *didn't realize*.
3 I don't mind talking about him *at all*.
4 We didn't know what it was *at the beginning*.
5 His intelligence is very *limited*.
6 He does have a lot of difficulty in *speaking*.
7 That must be very *disturbing* for him.
8 He *manages* very well.
9 What does he *like* doing?

10 He helps in the house *a bit*.
11 He loves to play snooker *for instance*.
12 How well can he *take care of* himself?
13 He'll put on two pairs of socks *rather than* one.
14 *Yet*, he can wash and dress himself.
15 Can he get about *by himself*?
16 He wouldn't be able to ask *for directions*.
17 Nobody would *be sure*.
18 One never really stops having *worries*.
19 He has a sort of *talent* for happiness.
20 Everybody's much more understanding about things *today*.

B In this conversation Pauline does most of the speaking. Teresa's role is to show Pauline that she is interested to hear about Andrew and wants her to continue talking. Making polite 'noises' is something you do automatically in your own language, and you may not be aware of what you actually do or say.

On the tape you heard Teresa using some of the 'noises' listed below for signifying her continued interest. Listen to the first part of the recording again and find the appropriate response to complete the conversation.

uhuh, oh dear, ah yes, oh, really, goodness, what a pity, mm, I see, no

1 Pauline She's trying to be an opera singer.
Teresa ...

2 Pauline He's mentally handicapped.
Teresa ...

3 Pauline It's Down's syndrome.
Teresa ...

4 Pauline It means that people sort of have some understanding that there's something wrong.
Teresa ...

5 Pauline He helps in the house a certain amount.
Teresa ...

Speaking

Look at the picture opposite and discuss in your group the problems disabled people face. Consider the following points:

how individuals can help
how the community can help
ways in which public facilities can be made more convenient for disabled
  people

"As far as I'm concerned it's neither public nor convenient."

GENTLEMEN

THE SPASTICS SOCIETY
It's not that people don't care, it's just that they don't think.

20 And later today

Listening

This recording is taken from a radio station. The announcer, with a few minutes to spare before the next part of the programme, gives the listeners some information about programmes for the rest of the morning.

Below is a transcription made by an audio-typist. She has made a number of mistakes. In some places she realized and put a question mark (?) or an omission sign (∧). Read the transcript carefully, noting places where you think a mistake might have been made, then listen to the recording and make the necessary corrections.

Studio production was by Brendan Donavan, and the editors were Francis Barnes and Eric Newton. Before the nine o'clock news, a quick look at one of this morning's headlines. At five to nine theirs Signs Tomorrow (?) with Jean Hook, and it's followed by The Wall Around Us, when we learn about antipodean curiosities, how the platypus wore his spure and why kangaroos are called joeys. That is Babies of the Pouch at nine thirty. After Tale at Ten, the first in a new ∧ (?) of theatrical profiles, with the title Waiting in the Wind. And this morning Ray Keeling talks to the ∧ old theatrical dame, Kitty Spurge.

(Excerpt)

Former (?) of Dame Kitty's colourful reminiscences, turn on at ten fifty for Waiting in the Wind. Later at two minutes past eleven, an examination of socialistic agricultural policis world ∧ when the Spectrum ∧ presents Let them eat Coke. Finally, at eleven forty nine, today is a concert, when the Bognor Philharmonic, ∧ the baton of Wanda van Ek will be bringing us Elgar Sea Songs sung by Evadne Butcher.

44

Practice

A Only ten of the words below occur in the recording. Put a tick (√) beside the ones you remember, then listen to the recording again to check your answers.

☐ production
☐ portraits
☐ editors
☐ serial
☐ studio
☐ features
☐ presents
☐ switch on
☐ credits
☐ group

scriptwriters ☐
tune in ☐
introduces ☐
direction ☐
set ☐
profiles ☐
series ☐
highlights ☐
team ☐
title ☐

B Each word in the first column above has a partner in the second. They do not necessarily mean the same thing, but would be found together. For example, both *production* and *direction* are aspects of making a programme. Link the word in the first column to its partner in the second. One has been done for you as an example. Use your dictionary to help you.

C The following nouns from Practice A all have a related verb. For example, *to direct* is the verb related to the noun *direction*. Use your dictionary to help you find the verbs related to the nouns below.

editors   highlights   serial   portrait   team   production

Speaking

Read the passage below silently and then discuss with your partner what it is, where you would see/hear it, and where the information would come from. Underline the stressed words and then read it aloud for your partner to check.

Tower Bridge is closed until early on Monday morning, so use London Bridge or Blackwall Tunnel. In Kent, Maidstone town centre's closed because of a carnival. Avoid that if you're driving. As you've heard, there's been motor racing at Brand's Hatch today, so expect very heavy traffic on the A20 between Dartford and Wrotham as the crowds leave. If you are going tomorrow and you want to join the M25 from the M1, leave the M1 at junction 7, the St Alban's exit, take the M10, then the A405, and the A6 to the M25 which you can join at South Mimms at junction 23.

21 Fairground Dream

Listening

Read the lyrics to the pop song below. Try to work out what the missing words are, then listen to the recording and find the missing words. Each gap represents one word.

FAIRGROUND DREAM

The fair was in town for a couple of days
One midsummer . . . . . . with the sky . . . . .
I . . . . . among the sideshows
When . . . . . .! I saw this vision.

Tall and smiling with an easy . . . . . .
The sunlight . . . . . . on his long blond hair
I felt a . . . . . . emotion
I had to . . . . . in closer.

There was . . . . . with him
That I . . . . . see
But when I came . . . . . up to him
I . . . . . . speak.

I . . . . . . him the whole fair through
The caterpillar and the dodgems . . . . .
Once close . . . . . . to touch him
I didn't have the . . . . . .

The . . . . . . it got, the less it felt real
I followed him onto the Ferris . . . . . .
We . . . . . the trees together
In separate . . . . . . again, though.

I saw his car stop . . . . . . me
He rejoined the . . . . . .
But when I got out of my car
He was . . . . . . to be found.

I didn't stop . . . . . . till I knew he'd gone
The wheel was black against the setting . . . . . .
He'd gone, he'd gone for . . . . . .
My fairground . . . . . . was over.

by Michael Scannell

Practice

A

Four verses of the song each have two lines that rhyme. The other three verses have lines that do not quite rhyme. Look at the words below, listen to the song again, and pair the words that rhyme by linking them with a line. Leave the words that do not rhyme. You should have four rhyming pairs at the end.

speak	real
days	through
found	hair
wheel	crowd
sun	see
air	ablaze
too	gone

B

Look at the six words below. Each one rhymes with two words in the circle. Using your dictionary to help you, group the words together according to rhyme.

see   speak   crowd   found   gone   sun

Speaking

In your group, discuss the following issues.

What are the ingredients of a successful pop song?
What are the qualities which produce an internationally famous pop star?
Why are some pop stars so wealthy?
Do you think that they deserve to earn so much?

22 What's on?

Listening

Every summer, Edinburgh, the capital city of Scotland, holds an international arts festival. In addition to the regular events, a great many other groups put on shows which are not part of the official festival. This is known as *The Fringe*.

Lizzie and Ben are in Edinburgh to go to as many of the events as they have time and money for. As there are about five hundred events, it is difficult to decide. They are in a pub discussing their plans for the following day. Look at the programme below, but do not read all the details. Only read the heavy print. Listen to the recording and find out where **Lizzie** decides to go. Where appropriate, put a tick (√) in the boxes provided on the programme.

THEATRE

☐ **BAHUMUTSI T.C. OF SOWETO, S.A.**
VENUE 35 Little Lyceum, Cambridge Street.
THE HUNGRY EARTH by Maishe Maponya. Excellent presentation of the history of S. Africa. Depicts the people's struggle against the system.
Aug 24–30 (not Sun.) 2.00 p.m. (3.20)   £2.50

☐ **CAMBRIDGE VAIN EMPIRES**
VENUE 8 Celtic Lodge, Brodies Close, Lawnmarket.
THE TEMPEST by William Shakespeare. 'Extraordinary: a savage Tempest, a mad Tempest ... fired by primitive magic and tribal rites ...' *Theatre Times.*
Aug 23–Sept 10 (not Sun.) 3.35 p.m. (5.25)   £1.80

☐ **OXFORD DRAMA PROGRAMMES**
VENUE 41 Masonic Lodge, 19 Hill Street.
TWELFTH NIGHT by William Shakespeare. International student company in new production from Oxford Festival.
Aug 23–27 12.45 p.m. (2.15)   £2.50

☐ **URGENT THEATRE, OXFORD**
VENUE 132 St Patrick's Primary School.
HEARTBREAKERS. A young boy gropes his way through adolescence into manhood: it is a painful and tragic journey. Powerful treatment of the loss-of-innocence theme.
Aug 18–Sept 3 (not Sun.) 9.30 p.m. (11.00)   £2.00

☐ **CAMBRIDGE UNIVERSITY THEATRE GROUP**
VENUE 12 Royal Overseas League, Princes St.
NEW ZONE WEST by Tony Lopez. Multi-media show incorporating lights, video, recorded sound and making and distributing artwork to the audience. An examination of the politics of art.
Aug 23–Sept 10 (not Sun.) Noon (12.45)   £1.00

COMEDY

☐ **THEATRE WORKSHOP COMPANY**
VENUE 35 Little Lyceum, Cambridge Street.
ACCIDENTAL DEATH OF AN ANARCHIST by Dario Fo. Disguise, lunacy and good humour are the ingredients of this grotesque farce.
Aug 17–Sept 3 (not Sun.) 7.30 p.m. (9.30)   £2.50
Sept 5–10   7.15 p.m. (9.15)

☐ **NEWSREVUE (STRODE-JACKSON)**
VENUE 7 Heriot Watt Theatre (Upstairs) Grindlay Street
NEWSREVUE 1983 Award winning satirical revue first seen on BBC 1. 'Brilliant'.
Aug 18–Sept 10 8.45 p.m. (10.15)   £2.50

EXHIBITIONS

☐ **COLIN BAXTER**
VENUE 1 Old Assembly Close, by Fringe Office
NEW LANDSCAPE PHOTOGRAPHS. A new venue for this popular exhibition which has already achieved great success at home and abroad.
Aug 13–Sept 10 10.00 a.m.–5.30 p.m.   Free

☐ **AMNESTY INTERNATIONAL**
VENUE 126 The Corner Stone, St John's Church
BOIAS FRIAS – images from Brazil. Two artists show drawings and water colours reflecting courage, stoicism and social satire. Mauricio Alvarez and Merlin Currie.
Aug 22–Sept 3 10.00 a.m.–7.00 p.m. (not Sun.) Free

MUSICALS

☐ **STUDIO THEATRE NEW YORK**
VENUE 44 Viewforth Centre, 104 Gilmore Place
YOU'RE A GOOD MAN, CHARLIE BROWN. Musical adaptation of Charles Shultz's popular cartoon strips. One of the United States' most successful musicals.
Aug 23–27 11.00 a.m. (12.30)   £1.50

MIME

☐ **DAVID GLASS MIME**
VENUE 3 Assembly Rooms, George St.
THE WHITE WOMAN. Exciting new mime from one of the genre's leading exponents. Set to the dynamic music of Grace Jones.
Aug 17–27 2.00 p.m. (3.35)   £2.50

ROCK, JAZZ, BLUES

☐ **MILLER AND FOWLER**
VENUE 61 Reid Concert Hall, Bristo Square
Local lads back in Edinburgh sounding better than ever. 'Dazzling', *Guitar* magazine.
Aug 21–Sept 3 (not Sun.) 8.00 p.m. (9.30)   £2.00

☐ **TOM ROBINSON AND CREW**
VENUE 3 Assembly Rooms, 54 George St.
SON OF A GUN. A late night musical extravaganza with Robinson and crew.
Aug 17–28 00.15 a.m. (1.30)   £3.00

Practice

A Listen to the recording again and find three ways of making suggestions.

1 . . . in the morning.
2 . . . that exhibition?
3 We . . . there for lunch.

B Find three ways in which Ben and Lizzie express agreement.

1 . . . . See you there at eleven.
2 . . . do that.
3 . . . go to that.

C Find two ways in which Ben indicates that he does not want to go to the mime.

1 Oh . . . mime!
2 I . . . mime.

Speaking

You and your boyfriend/girlfriend are on an English language course in Edinburgh during the festival. You have lessons every morning, but are free for the rest of the day. Your school runs a social programme and your course fee includes one coach outing, one theatre visit, and two sessions at the sports centre each week. Read through the week's programme below and discuss it with your partner. Decide which activities you want to attend, bearing in mind your individual interests, and that you have a limited amount of money.

	Monday	Tuesday	Wednesday	Thursday	Friday	Saturday	Sunday
Afternoon	Tennis 80p Swimming 60p Squash £1 available every day 2–9 p.m. Racquets and balls can be hired – details from Wendy. *Now doing reduced rates on Wednesdays*	Guided walk of the city to help you find your way around. Meet at reception at 2 p.m.	Visit to a whisky distillery. Coach leaves 2 p.m. outside main entrance. Tickets £4.00 in advance from Wendy (includes free tasting).	Visit to Edinburgh Castle. 12.30 p.m. – give names to Wendy. Pay at entrance (£1.50).	Visit to a woollen mill to see tartan being made. The mill has a shop where tartan is sold – good for souvenirs. Coach leaves 2 p.m. outside main entrance. Cost £5.00	All-day ramble in the Grampian Hills. Coach leaves 9 a.m. Tickets £5.00 in advance from Wendy (includes packed lunch).	Day trip to Loch Lomond. Coach leaves 8.30 a.m. Tickets £8.00 in advance from Wendy (includes 2-hour boat cruise).
Evening	Film on Edinburgh. Room 30 8 p.m. – Free *Extra showing 6 p.m.*	Visit to the Albion Theatre: *Mixed Doubles* (musical) 7.30 p.m. See Wendy for details. Cost £2.50	Disco Room 30 8 p.m. £2.00	Visit to Globe Theatre: *You're a good man, Charlie Brown* (musical comedy). 8 p.m. – details from Wendy. Cost £1.50	Visit to the world-famous Military Tattoo. Meet at reception 8.30 p.m. Cost £4.50	Shakespeare's *Twelfth Night* performed outside in Pavilion Gardens 7.45 p.m. Tickets £2.50 in advance from Wendy.	A visit to some typical old local pubs. Meet outside the White Horse, St James's Street 8 p.m. Free (excluding drinks!)

23 A Hollywood story

Listening

A In this recording, Blain, an actor, is telling a short, funny story about a friend of his. Below are the main points of the story, but in the wrong order. Listen to the recording and put the points in the correct order by placing the appropriate letter against the right number on the grid below. The first one has been done for you as an example.

a His agent rang him up.
b Tourists were allowed in the private areas.
c He went to Hollywood.
d Someone shouted that the tourists were coming.
e Blain has an Australian friend.
f All the tourists rushed in.
g What the tourists most wanted was to see a star.
h A tourist asked Blain's friend if he were a star.
i The stars would disappear.
j He was told he'd got a part in a Doris Day movie.
k On Blain's friend's first day he was having his lunch in the canteen.
l They were looking for a star.
m As soon as the tourists were seen approaching, the stars were warned.
n He was left alone in the canteen, apart from a couple of scene painters.
o Tours of the studio had been introduced to make some money.

1	e	6		11	
2		7		12	
3		8		13	
4		9		14	
5		10		15	

B Listen to the recording again, and mark (T) for true or (F) for false for the following sentences.

1 ☐ Blain's friend's name was Bruce.
2 ☐ The film he had a part in was *Pillow Talk*.
3 ☐ One of the stars of the film was Frank Sinatra.
4 ☐ The tourists realized that the stars were warned that they had arrived.
5 ☐ Blain's friend was the only person in the canteen who could have been a star.
6 ☐ Blain's friend knew why everybody was leaving the canteen.
7 ☐ Blain gives the impression that the tourists were young and female.
8 ☐ The point of the story is that the tourist doesn't recognize Blain's friend, but thinks he might be a star.

Practice

A To tell a story successfully, the narrator has to give enough information for the listener to understand the background of the story. He/she also has to keep the narrative moving and explain points he/she thinks the listener will need clarified.

Blain uses three methods to clarify his points:

a repetition
b emphasis and slowing down
c giving a word or phrase with a similar meaning

Listen to the recording again and put a, b, or c, in the boxes provided for the method Blain uses to clarify the topics below.

1 ☐ *Pillow Talk*
2 ☐ Rock Hudson
3 ☐ Doris Day
4 ☐ coach tours
5 ☐ what they really wanted
6 ☐ their recreation
7 ☐ in the canteen
8 ☐ all the actors

B Blain shows that he is aware of his listener in two ways: firstly, by using words to signal that an explanation is coming, and secondly, by directing remarks at him/her.

1 Find the word(s) Blain uses when he wants to signal an explanation about
a) *Pillow Talk*   b) the studios losing money.
2 Find the words Blain uses to include the listener when explaining the film *Pillow Talk*.

C   Blain employs a number of techniques to tell his story effectively. He uses a structure with *would* to express past habitual behaviour, which is typically used in narrative style (see Unit 12). Find examples of Blain's use of this structure.

Speaking

With a partner, make up a story (it need not be serious) in which each of the items pictured below is included. Consider the following points:

plot
background
use of direct speech for dramatic effect
the punchline

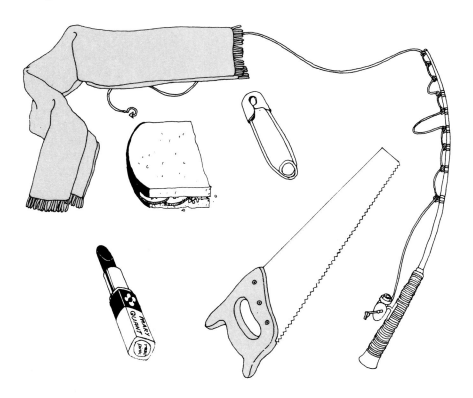